ALEX
AND
FRIENDS

ALEX
AND
FRIENDS

Animal Talk,
Animal Thinking

by **Dorothy Hinshaw Patent**

photographs by **William Muñoz**

Lerner Publications Company ■ Minneapolis

For Irene and Alex, of course!

We want to thank Irene Pepperberg, Diana May, the University of Arizona, Tucson, and all the birds and students who helped us with this project.

Photograph on p. 27 is reproduced through the courtesy of Diana May. Dialog between Lora Eston and Mrs. Eston on pp. 54–55 courtesy of TFH Publications, from *The Grey Parrot*, by W. De Grahl, 1987.

Website address: www.lernerbooks.com

Library of Congress Cataloging-in-Publication Data

Patent, Dorothy Hinshaw.
    Alex and friends : animal talk, animal thinking / by Dorothy Hinshaw Patent ; photographs by William Muñoz.
        p.   cm.
    Summary: Describes methods used by scientists to study how the brains of birds and other animals work and to determine whether animals can truly communicate verbally.
    ISBN 0-8225-2859-2 (alk. paper)
    1. Human-animal communication—Juvenile literature. [1. Animal communication. 2. Human-animal communication.]   I. Muñoz, William, ill. II. Title.
    QL776.P365 1998
    591.5—DC21   97–26496

Manufactured in the United States of America
1 2 3 4 5 6 – JR – 03 02 01 00 99 98

CONTENTS

1   A Very Special Parrot / 6

2   Using Sound to Communicate / 9

3   The Remarkable Parrot / 16

4   The African Grey Parrot / 25

5   Language—a Human Specialty? / 29

6   Talking Parrots / 50

7   Bird Smarts / 56

8   Other Aspects of Intelligence / 64

9   A Day in Irene's Life / 75

10   Into the Future / 81

     Glossary / 93

     Index / 94

Chapter 1

A Very Special Parrot

When parrots talk, they usually say silly things like "Polly want a cracker." They don't really know what they are saying. But there is one parrot who actually speaks more than a hundred words and understands their meaning. He is a grey parrot named Alex.

In order to understand what he says, Alex receives special training from scientist Irene Pepperberg. For almost 20 years, Alex has given Irene and other people a window into the brain of a bird. What Irene has found has surprised scientists around the world. Working with Alex, Irene has shown that at least one grey parrot has a very good brain, a brain that can accomplish many tasks we once thought only people—and maybe apes—could accomplish.

A Different Kind of Science

In the early 1970s, Irene was studying for a Ph.D. in chemical physics at Harvard University. One evening, she entertained herself by flipping on the TV and watching the then-new science show *Nova*. It changed her life. The program featured the topic of animal communication. It showed scientists using sign

Alex, a grey parrot, is the scientific subject and friend of scientist Irene Pepperberg.

language to communicate with chimpanzees, different scientists finding ways to communicate with dolphins, scientists studying singing whales, scientists studying the songs of birds. Irene was intrigued. She hadn't known such fascinating work with animals could be a part of science. While finishing up her degree, she attended classes in animal behavior and psychology, heard animal behavior scientists who came to local universities to discuss their work, and read books and articles in the library.

Irene had pet parakeets when she was a child, so she knew they could mimic the human voice. Why not get them to really talk, to say words and understand what the words meant? If chimps could make signs that indicated words, why couldn't parrots really talk?

Irene found that a couple of scientists had used methods related to natural parrot behavior to speed the birds' mimicking of words and phrases. The birds weren't learning the meanings of the words, however. Irene had some ideas about how to change the methods others used so that the parrots could connect meaning to the words.

After graduate school, Irene decided to try out her ideas in the laboratory. She went to a pet store and told the clerk she wanted a grey parrot. The clerk scooped Alex up out of a cage of eight, trimmed his beak, wings, and nails, and sold him to Irene for $600. After she got a government grant to begin her research with Alex, Irene was on her way to a completely different career than she would have had as a chemical physicist.

Chapter 2

Using Sound to Communicate

Parrots and people aren't the only creatures to communicate using sound. Animals from crickets to fish to wolves to monkeys get information across through sound.

Danger!

Warnings of predators are one of the most important forms of communication. If a California ground squirrel sees a hawk overhead, it lets out a whistle, which warns nearby squirrels of the danger. The sight of a predator on the ground, such as a rattlesnake, leads to a different, chattering call. But a faraway hawk may bring on a chatter, and a squirrel may whistle while running away from a pursuing ground predator, so the calls seem partially to indicate the degree of danger felt by the warning squirrel.

Some animals, however, have much more specific warning calls. Scientists Dorothy Cheney and Robert Seyfarth at the University of Pennsylvania studied vervet monkeys. First, the scientists recorded actual alarm calls the monkeys gave when they saw leopards, snakes, and eagles. Then, the scientists played back the calls to see how the monkeys behaved. When

Like ground squirrels, prairie dogs have separate calls to warn of different types of predators.

they heard a snake alarm, the monkeys looked around them in the grass. The eagle alarm made them look up in the air or run into the bushes. They climbed into the trees in response to the leopard call.

Birds also give alarm calls, sometimes specific ones. Bantam roosters have distinctly different alarm calls when presented with the videotaped image of a hawk as opposed to that of a raccoon. Scientists have noticed different alarm calls when observing a number of different wild birds, including jays and parrots.

Beautiful Bird Songs

The most familiar sounds humans hear from wild animals are the beautiful songs of wild birds. Some birds, like canaries, have become popular pets as much because of their lovely singing as their pretty feathers. When a bird sings, it's communicating messages. But messages about what?

The most familiar bird songs are those of male birds during the breeding season. Many songbirds travel south in the fall and spend the winter in areas of mild climate. In the spring, they return to the same vicinity where they lived the previous summer. Each male songbird sets up an area, called a territory, in which he and his mate build a nest and raise a family. He perches on branches near the territory boundary and sings the song typical of his kind, announcing that this is his home and others of his species had better stay away. If another male challenges him, he will chase the intruder away.

Bantam cross roosters also have special calls to warn of hawks or ground-based predators like raccoons.

Many songbirds must learn how to put sounds together to create the vocalizations typical of the species. During the natural course of events, a male songbird chick hears his father's voice as he grows up. He also hears plenty of other bird sounds. However, scientists Peter Marler and S. Peters of Rockefeller University found that young songbirds learn the song of their own kind easily. Marler and Peters raised young swamp sparrows in the laboratory and played tape recordings of swamp sparrow songs. They also played tapes of song sparrow songs rearranged to make them more similar to those of swamp sparrows. The young birds learned only the songs of their own species, ignoring the song sparrow elements. But if the young sparrow has a sole companion of another species, he may come to sing that species' song. Interaction with other birds is very important when a sparrow is learning to sing.

Other birds are more flexible in their learning. Some, such as mockingbirds, actually learn the songs of other birds and may let out a long stream of beautiful singing that mixes in songs of several different species. Their mimicry is so exact that even electronic analysis can't detect differences from the original. Besides copying as many as 39 different species songs and 50 call notes, some mockingbirds can bark like a dog, cackle like a hen, or "play" notes that sound like a piano.

"Talking" Birds

Mockingbirds aren't the only expert mimics in the bird world. A number of members of the crow and starling families, in addition to the more familiar parrots, can be startling mimics. Captive Eurasian jays have learned to bark at the sight of a dog and meow when they see a cat, as well as scold their owners by repeating words the owners had used with them. Some birds, such as the mynah and many parrots, have become popular pets because of their talent at copying human speech.

Anecdotes abound from people surprised by the mimicking talent of their captive birds. Some of these hint at the possibility that perhaps birds can do more than just mindlessly copy sounds they've heard. Many a pet bird has surprised its owner by using words appropriately and combining them in what seem like meaningful ways. A good example is Arnie, a starling named after the popular hero of the book, *Arnie the Darling Starling*. This Arnie belongs to Judy Hoy, a wildlife rehabilitator who lives in Montana. Judy has cared for injured and otherwise needy wild animals for many years. She has observed much of what looks like intelligent behavior from the birds she has tended.

When Arnie came along, Judy was reluctant to take care of him. The starling is an invader from Europe and sometimes takes over nesting sites from native North American birds. Many people consider starlings to be pests. But the little boy who brought Arnie in was so concerned for his welfare that Judy agreed to take care of the baby bird.

Captive starlings have been known to mimic human speech, usually beginning around seven months of age. Arnie began at four months and hasn't stopped since. Judy has many stories about how Arnie has combined words appropriately into sentences he's never heard before. When Judy would enter the room where Arnie's box was kept, she'd say, "Hi, Arnie, what are you doing?" Or, "Hi, Arnie, you're a good bird, I love you." Not surprisingly, Arnie learned to say, "Hi, Arnie," and would do so when Judy arrived. But then Judy said to him, "I'm Judy, you're Arnie. You are supposed to say, 'Hi, Judy.'" After that, Arnie would say, "Hi, Judy," instead of "Hi, Arnie." He would also say, "I love you, Judy," although no one had

Arnie and Judy Hoy carry on a conversation.

ever spoken that sentence in his presence. All he had heard was "I love you, Arnie."

Another time, Judy came into the room to feed a young swallow that was kept across the room from Arnie. Arnie said, "Hi, Judy," and she answered, "Hi, Arnie," without a second thought. "What are you doing?" Arnie then asked. "I'm feeding a little bird," answered Judy. Arnie answered, "Arnie is a little bird." Judy was amazed. She had never heard Arnie use the word "little" before. What he said, and the way he said it—in a tone of voice like a child with hurt feelings—seemed to be a bid for attention from Judy.

The best known and most popular bird mimics are parrots and their smaller relatives, parakeets and conures. Most of these birds can learn to mimic the human voice, bringing entertainment to their owners. Largely for this reason, members of the parrot family are the third most popular pet, after cats and dogs. Around the world, millions of parrots are kept as pets.

Chapter 3

The Remarkable Parrot

As I strolled down the path toward Lake Petén Itzá in Guatemala, I heard raucous cries over my left shoulder. I looked up and saw a flock of bright green parrots flapping their way toward a tall tree, squawking all the way. The flock alighted in the tree, and the birds disappeared into the bright green foliage. But I could still hear their croaky chattering. Parrots are rarely silent when they are together.

Parrots around the World

Parrots have it all—beauty, intelligence, and personality. They come in a rainbow of colors, from the brilliant blue hyacinth macaw to the delicate pink Moluccan cockatoo. Some, like the rainbow lorakeet, have patches of different bright colors splashed over their wings and bodies. The majority of parrots are bright green, which provides effective camouflage among the leaves of forest trees.

Most of the over three hundred parrot species live in the American tropics and Australia, with others in Africa and Asia. In most species, males and females look alike. The feet and beaks of parrots are specially adapted for feeding on nuts and seeds. Each foot has four toes, with two pointing forward and the other two pointing backward. The feet are especially agile.

Macaws, like the military macaw, can be tamed and kept as pets, if people are willing to spend time with them.

Kinds of Parrots

Many kinds of parrots are kept as pets, but they are still wild animals. Only the familiar budgerigar, or budgie, has truly been domesticated. Budgies were first raised in captivity in 1840. The wild species is mostly green, but breeders have produced a rainbow of budgie colors—yellow, sky blue, white, cobalt blue, and others.

Parrots belong to a family that scientists call the Psittacidae. Within this family are smaller subgroups. Most familiar types, such as lovebirds, macaws, conures, parrotlets, and parakeets, are in the largest subgroup.

Macaws, which live in South America, Central America, and parts of Mexico, are the biggest type of parrot. The largest of all, the brilliant blue hyacinth macaw, is about 40 inches (100 cm) long from beak to tail tip. Macaws are intelligent birds with very loud voices and long, pointed tails.

Lovebirds, on the other hand, are heavy bodied but small—all less than 7 inches (18 cm) long. These affectionate birds live mostly in Africa and on the island of Madagascar.

Lories and lorakeets, which live in Indonesia, New Guinea, Australia, and on Pacific islands, are in another group. They differ from typical parrots in a number of ways. While they are popular as pets because of their brilliant greens, blues, reds, and yellows, these birds are somewhat difficult to keep because of their feeding habits. Instead of using their hooked beaks to pry apart nuts and fruits, lories and lorakeets feed mostly on honey and pollen that they mop up with the fringed tip of their tongue.

Conures are small, slender birds with long, pointed tails. They live in Central and South America and northward into parts of Mexico. The extinct Carolina parakeet was a species of conure.

True parakeets are a widespread group of birds found mostly in Asia and Australia. Most parakeets are small and have long, pointed tails. The budgie is a species of parakeet.

Many pet parrots belong to the Amazon parrots that live wild in the tropical parts of the Americas. Amazons have stout green bodies and short square or rounded tails. Their bodies and heads are often marked with red, yellow, or blue. The yellow-headed Amazon is a popular pet because it talks well.

Cockatoos, which live in Australia and nearby islands, belong to a different subgroup. There are just 16 kinds of cockatoos. These large birds with especially powerful beaks are popular in captivity because of the graceful feathery crests on their heads and their cuddly personalities.

The rest of the parrot family are less familiar to most people. One subgroup has only one species, the flightless New Zealand kakapo. Unlike most parrots, the kakapo is active at night. It is also called the owl parrot because the feathers on its face form a disk around the eyes, just as owl feathers do. New Zealand is also home to another subgroup with only two species, the kaka and the kea. The keas are strange birds with long, pointed beaks. They are quite fearless and aggressive and sometimes are reported to attack sheep. Pygmy parrots live only in New Guinea and nearby islands. They are all less than 4 inches (10 cm) long. They feed on funguses instead of nuts and seeds.

Most cockatoos, such as the greater sulfur-crested cockatoo, are beautiful birds with graceful crests.

The budgie is the only truly domesticated parrot and comes in many colors.

When a parrot eats, it stands on one foot and holds the food in the other while it uses its lower beak to peel off the tough coat of seeds and nuts. Parrots develop a preference for one foot, being either left-footed or right-footed.

Intelligence Comes Naturally

One evening at the edge of a Guatemalan clearing, my husband and I enjoyed watching a pair of spectacular parrots called scarlet macaws in a tree right over our heads. Their elegant beauty took our breath away, but their behavior made us laugh. It was almost impossible not to compare them to a human couple having an argument. One bird squawked with a complaining tone and reached out with one of its powerfully clawed feet to grab the other. They pawed at each other and swung around the branch, taking turns "scolding." Finally one bird flew off to another tree and "complained" to its mate from a distance. After a few moments, the other macaw joined it, and the two birds rubbed their beaks together while making soft noises. We couldn't help thinking they were making up after a fight.

Like humans, parrots are very social, and also like us, the male and female forge a strong bond that can last for life. Parrots have other parallels to humans, too. They live for a long time—50 to 100 years—and they tend to eat a varied diet. These three traits—a varied diet, a long life, and an active social life, are all factors linked to high intelligence in the animal kingdom.

Think about it. If an animal consumes a varied diet, it has to be able to recognize many different kinds of food and to tell when each one is ready to be eaten. A parrot needs to remember where it found food in the past and how to make its way to different food sources. Some macaws feed on hundreds of different kinds of trees that may be scattered over many miles throughout the forest. Finding these sorts of foods requires the ability to learn and to remember, both important aspects of intelligence.

Intelligence is important to a long-lived animal, too. The longer one lives, the more variation there will be in the environment over the years. One year may be hot and dry while another could be cool and wet. Such different environmental conditions will favor different plants, causing even greater variation in what is available to eat. A long life provides plenty of time for learning. Animals that live many years, such as elephants and parrots, tend to have fewer inborn behaviors and more learned ones. That way, they can more easily adapt to changes that can occur over the years in their environments.

Social life also requires intelligence. An individual living socially has to be able to communicate with others in the group. The ability to communicate complex or subtle messages is an important component of intelligence. An animal may make a loud sound as a threat to another animal, for example. Then another aspect of intelligence kicks in—the other animal needs to interpret the intended message. Was that a threat or merely an attempt to attract attention? Or maybe it had another meaning altogether. Then the second animal must respond in an appropriate way to the action of the first, based on its interpretation of the message, and so forth.

Parrots as Pets

Parrots make fine pets for people because they are so much like us. They need an active social life to be content, and they readily form bonds of affection with humans. A parrot can become a lifelong companion and friend, since the life span of some species is about the same as ours. As one enthusiastic parrot owner explains in the Nature TV program *Parrots—Look Who's*

Nicki, a chattering lory, is good friends with Adell Coon.

Talking, "It's like having another person in the house, except it has feathers."

Some kinds of parrots are excellent mimics and learn to "talk" with ease. Usually, they just repeat words and phrases they have learned, with no indication that they understand what those words and phrases mean. But people who own parrots often find that their pets use some words in appropriate ways, at least understanding that the particular combination of sounds might affect the bird's owner to bring about behavior the parrot wants. Take Nicki, for example, a chattering lory from Australia who belongs to Adell and Don Coon of Hamilton, Montana. Nicki lives in a big cage filled with toys. But he prefers being loose in the house. When he is put in his cage, Nicki pleads to be released, "Let me out." If that doesn't work, he says, "Please." If Adell refuses to let him out, saying "I'm busy," Nicki keeps on begging by uttering, "Nicki be good."

Sometimes, Nicki also appears to try to talk to other animals. Once Don and Adell acquired two marmots, large chunky relatives of squirrels. Nicki was very curious about the marmots hiding in a box. "What are you?" he said. They didn't come

Nicki entertains himself with games, like playing with a plastic ball.

Nicki invented his own 'chase the Frisbee' game.

out. "Come here," he commanded. Still no response. Nicki gave up, saying, "Lost ya."

Because of their intelligence and willingness to please, parrots can be taught all sorts of tricks besides talking. They can learn to dance and sing, to play ball, and to open and close doors. They can invent their own games, too. Nicki devised his own version of a fetching game. He took a flat plastic top of the sort you might find on a can of nuts and used it as a Frisbee. In this game, Nicki throws the "Frisbee" from his beak with a fling of his head. Adell fetches it, then throws it again for Nicki, and so forth. Like a retrieving dog, Nicki will play this game on and on until his human friend tires of it.

A Lifelong Friend

Parrots can be wonderful pets and playful companions. But because of their emotional needs and their long life, pet parrots are also a big responsibility. Parrots that don't get a lot of attention from their owners become emotionally disturbed, just like badly neglected human children. Many zoos have areas the public doesn't see that house pet birds rejected by their owners.

Having parrots around is like having children at home who never grow up. They stay emotionally attached to their owners and don't transfer that attachment to other people well. Fortunately, Nicki is adaptable and goes with Adell and Don during their summer work in the woods, where Nicki enjoys exploring the forest floor. Nights in the mountains are cold, so Nicki worms his way down to the bottom of Adell's sleeping bag to keep warm, nibbling at her toes in the night if she crowds him. Adell Coon loves Nicki very much. But she says if she'd known just how big a responsibility he was going to be, she might not have decided to buy him.

Chapter 4

The African Grey Parrot

When Irene Pepperberg got the idea to teach a parrot to understand and speak English words so she could have a window into the brain of a bird, the African grey parrot *(Psittacus erithacus erithacus)* was the obvious choice. This species is universally accepted as the best mimic of human speech. Because they are so intelligent and are such good mimics, grey parrots were the third most commonly traded wild bird species in the world between 1983 and 1989.

Alex, a typical African grey parrot

Greys can master human speech so well that humans can easily mistake the bird's voice for that of a person. One German owner of a grey parrot got a good laugh when she brought her beloved pet along on a train trip. She placed his cage on the luggage rack above the seats and settled in for the journey. A couple of women joined her in the compartment, chatting loudly. When the conversation paused, the women were shocked to hear a sweet, childlike voice from above speaking loving words. They turned on the bird's owner, accusing her. "What? You dare to leave your poor child up there on the luggage rack instead of taking it on your lap? Well, I never——!" After she controlled her laughter, the owner brought down the cage and showed her traveling companions the "child" in the cage, and they all had a laugh together.

The African Grey Parrot in the Wild

The African grey parrot lives in the tropical forests of Sierra Leone, and southeastern Guinea inland through northwestern Tanzania and western Kenya. Greys prefer forested areas along rivers. The grey parrot is not an endangered species. A 1995 study estimated that 600,000 live in the wild. However, logging has reduced the habitat available to the bird in much of its natural range. Old trees are important to the birds because they contain the holes the birds need for nesting cavities.

During the late 1980s, almost 350,000 grey parrots were exported from Africa, and exports have continued into the 1990s. No one knows how many greys can safely be captured without dangerously reducing populations of the species.

The plumage of the common variety of grey parrot is mostly pale grey, with bare whitish skin around the eyes, dark grey wing feathers, and a bright red tail that is spread in flight. A rare variety is darker overall, with a lighter beak and maroon tail feathers. The grey parrot is about the size of a pigeon, weighing about 14 to 17 ounces, with males slightly larger than females. The eyes of a young bird are black, turning to grey as it gets older, and finally to yellow. A grey parrot in captivity can live as long as 70 years. More typically, greys live 20 to 25 years.

Living Wild

Unfortunately, very little is known about the life of grey parrots in the wild. The breeding season varies depending on where

Grey parrots in the wild

the birds live. Like most parrots, greys construct their nests in tree holes. The female usually lays two to five eggs. While she sits on the eggs to keep them warm, the male feeds her several times a day. After the chicks hatch, the female apparently feeds them at first, with the male joining in later. The young are ready to leave the nest when they are about 80 days old.

Grey parrots are highly social. When the birds aren't breeding, they travel in large, raucous flocks that roost together at night. In the early morning, even before dawn, a flock leaves its roosting trees and heads out looking for food. Grey parrots feed mostly on the buds, flowers, fruits, and nuts of a variety of trees.

Like other parrots, greys are very noisy. Wild grey parrots make many different sounds, ranging from harsh squawks to melodious whistles. Because they are usually seen in big groups, it is difficult to single out the voice of an individual bird. Recently, three Belgian scientists carefully analyzed a sound recording of a pair of wild grey parrots and found that the birds' vocalizations included mimicry of the calls of nine different bird species and a bat.

Greys in History

The Romans apparently kept parrots for pets, as the Roman moralist, Cato the Censor, criticized people for carrying parrots around on their hands. Romans received at least one large shipment of parrots from Africa, which were eaten at banquets and fed to the lions. Grey parrots were probably among them.

The first scientific description of the grey came from an Italian naturalist in the mid-1500s, so they've been known by Western scientists for more than four hundred years. In past times, pet parrots were popular with royalty; King Henry VIII of England, who ruled from 1509 to 1547, had a captive grey.

Chapter 5

Language—a Human Specialty?

Other animals may use sound to communicate, but humans have carried the art of social communication to an extreme through our use of language. Human languages provide an amazing flexibility to communicate about almost anything. Many scientists believe that human language is so much more

People use spoken language to convey all sorts of information. Here, a volunteer describes the debris she has collected during the Shedd Aquarium beach cleanup in Chicago to another volunteer, who writes down the information.

complex than any other animal system of communication that it is a special talent limited to our species. They insist that the word *language* be applied only to the ways in which humans use words to communicate. Animals may communicate, they say, but not through true language.

Dr. Noam Chomsky of the Massachusetts Institute of Technology is perhaps the world's foremost linguist. He believes that language is unique to humans and that it comes naturally to us

Chomsky and Language Understanding

Noam Chomsky was born in Philadelphia in 1928. His father studied historical linguistics, so Chomsky was exposed to language study from an early age.

Before Chomsky, linguists had concentrated mainly on describing the world's many languages. Chomsky found ways to try to explain how languages worked. His first book, published in 1957, was entitled *Syntactic Structures* and examined aspects of grammar.

Children learn language naturally through their interactions with other humans, and they master this complex subject quickly. All children go through the same stages of language learning. Chomsky explains these facts by saying that all children are born with the knowledge of language's basic structure. This knowledge, he believes, is held somewhere in a special part of the human brain possessed by no other species.

Many linguists agree with Chomsky's ideas. The following quote, from the introduction to a textbook, summarizes their beliefs:

because our brains are unique. Chomsky has many followers and many critics. He stated his beliefs clearly in one interview:

"Humans can fly about 30 feet—that's what they do in the Olympics. Is that flying? The question is totally meaningless." Chomsky goes on to say that trying to teach animals such as chimpanzees to use language is like trying to teach people to fly—we don't have wings, so we can't really fly, even though we can soar through the air for a limited distance. Likewise, says

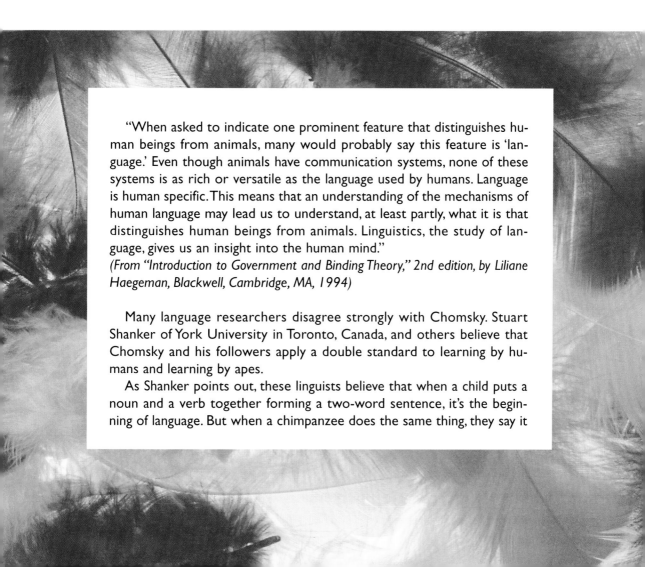

"When asked to indicate one prominent feature that distinguishes human beings from animals, many would probably say this feature is 'language.' Even though animals have communication systems, none of these systems is as rich or versatile as the language used by humans. Language is human specific. This means that an understanding of the mechanisms of human language may lead us to understand, at least partly, what it is that distinguishes human beings from animals. Linguistics, the study of language, gives us an insight into the human mind."
(From "Introduction to Government and Binding Theory," 2nd edition, by Liliane Haegeman, Blackwell, Cambridge, MA, 1994)

Many language researchers disagree strongly with Chomsky. Stuart Shanker of York University in Toronto, Canada, and others believe that Chomsky and his followers apply a double standard to learning by humans and learning by apes.

As Shanker points out, these linguists believe that when a child puts a noun and a verb together forming a two-word sentence, it's the beginning of language. But when a chimpanzee does the same thing, they say it

Chomsky, animals other than humans can't use language, since they lack the "language organ" he believes lies somewhere in the human brain.

Teaching Animals Language

Those who disagree with Chomsky have worked with animals such as chimpanzees to show that they can master the rudi-

has nothing to do with language. Humans and chimpanzees are very closely related biologically. No one should be surprised if our close relatives share the beginnings of language understanding with us.

Other scientists reject the idea that there is a unique "language organ" in the human brain. Helen Neville at the University of Oregon in Eugene studied language learning in children and second language learning in adults. She found that up to the age of four or five, children process language all over the brain. After that, vocabulary words tend to be processed in parts of both the left and right halves of the brain. Words that provide information about grammar and syntax, however, are processed in a limited region of the left half of the brain. When adults learn a second language, the grammar words do not become associated with the specialized grammar region of the brain—their grammar knowledge is not limited to a single area, yet they are capable of speaking, reading, and writing the other language.

Elizabeth Bates of the University of California, San Diego, has shown that the brains of children with brain damage can reorganize without losing any specific function, including language. Undamaged parts can take over the functions once handled by damaged parts. The children are not

ments of language. During the 1960s and 1970s, a number of scientists experimented with the chimpanzee's possible language skills. The first efforts to work with chimps met with failure because chimpanzees don't have a vocal apparatus that enables them to form words. But in 1966, Beatrix and R. Allen Gardner of the University of Nevada began raising a 10-month-old chimpanzee named Washoe as if she were a human

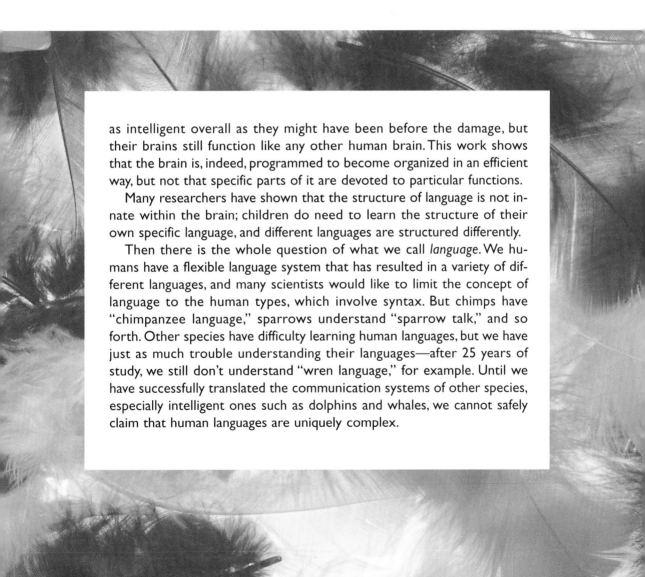

as intelligent overall as they might have been before the damage, but their brains still function like any other human brain. This work shows that the brain is, indeed, programmed to become organized in an efficient way, but not that specific parts of it are devoted to particular functions.

Many researchers have shown that the structure of language is not innate within the brain; children do need to learn the structure of their own specific language, and different languages are structured differently.

Then there is the whole question of what we call *language*. We humans have a flexible language system that has resulted in a variety of different languages, and many scientists would like to limit the concept of language to the human types, which involve syntax. But chimps have "chimpanzee language," sparrows understand "sparrow talk," and so forth. Other species have difficulty learning human languages, but we have just as much trouble understanding their languages—after 25 years of study, we still don't understand "wren language," for example. Until we have successfully translated the communication systems of other species, especially intelligent ones such as dolphins and whales, we cannot safely claim that human languages are uniquely complex.

Animals from chimpanzees to pigeons can learn to recognize categories such as 'dog,' even when the category includes very different looking examples.

child, including exposing her to language. Instead of trying to get Washoe to form spoken words, the Gardners used a modified version of American Sign Language (ASL), which is used by deaf people to communicate. Arm and hand movements substitute for words. For example, the word fruit is expressed by placing one fist alongside the mouth. Whenever the Gardners entered the trailer where Washoe lived, they communicated between themselves as well as with her by way of ASL. They used it just as human parents would use spoken language with a child, to point out pictures in books and to identify objects and actions.

Washoe learned many of the skills a human child masters.

She got herself dressed and undressed, ate with a spoon, drank from a cup, and used the toilet. She enjoyed thumbing through picture books and playing with her doll. She also learned to "talk" in the same way a human child would, by imitating the adults who shared her world. Washoe was encouraged to form the ASL signs for words correctly, much as a human child is encouraged by its parents to pronounce words correctly. On her own, Washoe began to combine the signs in what seemed to be meaningful ways. When she heard a dog bark, she signed "listen dog." She called her doll "baby mine."

Like a human child, Washoe generalized her knowledge beyond her first encounters. She could recognize a dog as a dog, whether it was big or small, black or white. Sometimes she generalized in unusual ways. After learning the sign for *flower*, she generalized it to various odors, including cigar smoke, rather than to other flowers.

After 51 months of training, Washoe could use at least 132 signs in a reliable way. The Gardners' work was greeted with great enthusiasm by the popular press, with articles in magazines and newspapers speculating wildly about the possibilities of animal-human communication.

Criticism of the Gardners

Other scientists, however, had problems with the Gardners' work. Scientists generally strive to conduct their work in a very objective way, following certain rules of procedure. Science proceeds in one of two ways. Scientists plan experiments and repeat them over and over again, only considering the results positive if they get the same results a number of times. If experimental methods aren't appropriate, they observe natural phenomena in an objective and detached way. The Gardners used neither of these methods. Scientific objectivity wasn't their goal. They avoided rigid experiments on purpose—after all, what parents would experiment on their developing children? Detached observation was also out of the question. In order to be treated like a human child, Washoe had to interact with her human "parents" and "friends" in much the same emotional way a child would. The Gardners could watch Washoe talk to her doll or to other animals, but of course, her communication with humans was the most important part of what was going on.

Criticism of the Gardners' work on scientific grounds misses the point of what they did. Their goal was to investigate the intellectual capacity of a chimpanzee and to compare it with humans, and language is an integral part of human intelligence. In addition, teaching Washoe to "talk" gave the Gardners a win-

When chimpanzees are raised by people, like this orphaned youngster at Lowry Park Zoo in Tampa, Florida, they can become very tame.

dow into her mind, a window unlike anything that preceded it.

It is true that criticism is an important part of how science progresses. One job of a scientist is to study the experiments of colleagues, find possible weaknesses, and suggest improvements. But because the Gardners' endeavor was so unusual, some scientists in the areas of animal behavior and intelligence had a field day tearing their work apart. The importance of what they had done—finding a way of communicating directly with another species—got completely lost.

Fortunately, criticism didn't stop the Gardners. They expanded their efforts, using other chimps and getting other scientists involved. In addition, several laboratories experimented with different methods of studying chimpanzees and language. Some tried to get around the lack of objectivity that comes with ASL. When two individuals communicate by ASL, they are by definition interacting with one another. That makes complete objectivity impossible. Also, interpreting the signs made by a chimp can lead to problems. An investigator who expects the chimp to respond in a certain way might believe the animal was making a particular sign when actually it was just waving its arms about in excitement. It was also possible that, in directly interacting with the chimps, the scientists were giving unconscious hints as to what response they expected.

Other Chimp Research

A flurry of research followed the initial criticisms of the Gardners' work. In the early 1980s, the scientific establishment concluded that certain chimpanzees had *not* shown any real use of language; they were merely imitating their human companions. Language, the scientists decided, was beyond the ability of apes, and studying the subject was therefore a waste of time.

Meanwhile, Drs. Duane and Sue Savage-Rumbaugh of the Language Research Center at Georgia State University quietly continued their studies. They had developed another way of getting at the possible language understanding of animals. Instead of ASL, their chimps used a keyboard with dozens of buttons, each marked with a geometric symbol. Each symbol, called a lexigram, stood for an object or action, just like a word. The chimps learned to use the keyboard to communicate with the scientists, who were in a different room. The keyboard eliminated the problem of interpretation of signs—either the animal chose the right key or it didn't.

The Rumbaugh team worked with a number of chimpanzees. One, named Lana, learned about 100 symbols for objects such as can, shoe, and cup, and colors such as purple, red, and black. She also used her keyboard vocabulary to ask for things for which she didn't have words. She described a cucumber as "banana which is green" and an orange as the "apple which is orange (color)."

Two other chimps, Sherman and Austin, developed another language skill that showed they really understood the meanings of the lexigrams. First, Sherman and Austin learned to classify some items into two categories—food and tools. Once the chimps got the idea that familiar items could be identified as either foods or tools, the chimps were taught two new lexigrams, one that meant tool and another meaning food. Finally, they were asked to label 17 previously learned lexigrams for foods (and drinks) and tools as belonging to the correct category. The chimps made only one mistake—Sherman called a sponge a *food* instead of a *tool*. But this error is understandable, as he would use a sponge to soak up favorite juices, then suck on it as if it were something to eat.

Chimps are always curious and can get in trouble for it.

Kanzi

During the 1980s, the team at Georgia State decided to experiment with a different kind of chimpanzee, the bonobo. The bonobo is a rare and endangered animal that seems even closer to humankind than the common chimp. Bonobos are more likely to walk on two legs than common chimps, they use eye contact to get another's attention, and they seem to communicate more readily by gestures and vocalizations.

The first efforts with a bonobo were discouraging. Matata lived wild until she was six years old. After years of work, she could not understand the idea of using lexigrams as symbols for real physical objects. But during her laboratory sessions, Matata was accompanied by her young adopted son, Kanzi.

Kanzi picked up the idea of the keyboard by watching Matata struggle with the system. Kanzi was trained further, through walks in the forest rather than in laborious hours of boring, repetitive laboratory sessions. People spoke to him as if he could understand words, and the lexigrams on the keyboard were paired with the spoken words so he could learn that a lexigram stood for a word. Kanzi was encouraged to use the lexigrams to ask for favorite activities, like videotapes, games, and food.

By the age of six, Kanzi had mastered about two hundred lexigrams. He also combined them, sometimes adding gestures, to make simple sentences. Kanzi appears to understand human speech, too.

Dr. Sue Savage-Rumbaugh and her colleagues believe that their work shows bonobos can understand language about as well as a two-and-a-half-year-old child. Kanzi's understanding is better than his ability to produce language. He can "talk" at about the level of a one-and-a-half-year-old child. With humans, too, language understanding is much easier than language production. A young child understands much more than he or she can say. When Kanzi was tested in parallel with a two-year-old girl named Alia, they both showed they understood what was being asked of them with respect to a number of different kinds of requests, such as "Take the can opener to the bedroom" and "Go to the microwave and get the tomato."

The term *syntax* is used to describe the inner structure or grammar of a language. A key to the question of whether animals actually use language is whether they understand the syntax, or structure. Critics of work involving ASL comment that the signing chimps don't use syntax reliably; they don't always put the words in the same order. In ASL, however, word order doesn't have the same importance as in spoken English.

To see if a chimp could comprehend syntax, Kanzi and Alia were tested on word reversal requests, such as "Put the raisins in the shoe" and "Put the shoe in the raisins." Both the chimp and the child scored well on these tests, showing that they understood the importance of word order in giving meaning to a sentence. That means they had some limited concept of syntax. Kanzi actually scored higher than Alia in the tests. But many scientists are still not impressed. They say that what Kanzi and other chimps do still cannot be considered language.

What Is Language?

A large part of the problem is that people can't seem to agree on a precise definition for the word "language." No scientist would argue that animals like chimpanzees, dolphins, or parrots could use language to write poetry or describe the structure of the atom. But that doesn't mean that their brains cannot grasp the concept of using language to communicate messages to others. As Dr. Sue Savage-Rumbaugh states, "Though none will argue that any animal has the full capacity of humans for language, none should deny that at least some animals have quite impressive competencies for language skills, including speech comprehension."

In human languages, some words describe objects. They are called nouns. Other words, called verbs, describe actions. Still other words fulfill secondary roles such as modifying nouns (adjectives such as hot, yellow, or beautiful) or verbs (adverbs like warmly, quickly, or angrily). Still others play more minor roles.

Linguistic communication involves the use of symbols—words—to represent objects and actions. When we use the word *ball*, for example, we form a mental picture of something round. We recognize the word as a stand-in for the object. If we tell someone, "Roll the ball," we expect him or her to place the ball in motion along a surface such as the floor. The word *roll* is a symbol for the action of placing the ball in motion along a surface. "Throw the ball" means something quite different. To understand how language works is to know that words are symbols for specific objects and actions.

The key question is, when a chimpanzee signs "Give orange," does it understand that the symbol *orange* means the delicious fruit and the symbol *give* means the act of someone handing the fruit over? Or does the animal simply know that signing "Give orange" results in getting the fruit? If the chimp really understands that *give* represents an action and *orange* represents an object, then one could say that the animal has some understanding of words as symbols.

Beyond Chimpanzees

Some scientists decided to work with species other than chimpanzees to investigate the possibilities of language understanding in animals. They wanted to see if animals could understand new sentences using words they had already learned. If they could, it would help answer the criticism that animals like Washoe were just memorizing strings of words like "gimme orange" and not understanding how words can be put together to make unique sentences. In the 1980s, researchers showed that dolphins, sea lions, and parrots could learn to understand unique sentences.

Still, linguists like Chomsky have not been swayed. They are convinced that the chimps and other animals don't really comprehend language, no matter how they may perform in experiments. According to Chomsky, the animals cannot be using the same part of their brains to communicate, since his theory says only humans have the "language organ." But no one has yet located this structure within the brain; it exists only in theory.

Even if animals do lack a unique "language organ" lodged somewhere in the human brain, they are still capable of learning some basic aspects of communication through human-

California sea lions are intelligent animals that are easy to train. Some sea lions have learned to understand commands they have never heard, much like dolphins.

devised symbols. The argument as to whether this usage is truly language or not misses an important question: How are all these animals, with differently organized brains, able to perform these tasks so well? Do they have "organs" specialized for their style of communication?

Upping the Ante

Scientists like Dr. Sue Savage-Rumbaugh became frustrated by the criticisms of their work. The critics seemed to keep changing their standards for what constitutes "true language." At first, language was the ability to understand the symbolic nature of words and use them to communicate. Once animals showed they could understand and use words about as well as a young human child, the definitions seem to have changed.

One claim is that the animals don't really understand what

What Dolphins Can Learn

When ape language experiments were in full swing, one serious criticism was that experimenters couldn't tell if the animals really understood what they were "saying." Maybe a chimp signing *banana* just knew that if it moved its arms in a particular way, someone would hand it a banana. It might not know that the sign stood for the piece of fruit. Also, the apes often didn't pay attention to the order of the "words" they used when producing language. In English, the word order is very important to the meaning of language. "The dog bit the man" means something very different from "the man bit the dog."

To get around this problem, scientist Louis Herman at the University of Hawaii decided to study dolphins in the 1980s. He focused on the animals' ability to follow commands rather than on their ability to produce language. Herman chose dolphins because they are intelligent, highly social animals that use sound both for communication and for finding their way around. Also, dolphins are highly trainable; their performances are very popular at aquariums and sea parks.

Herman worked with two dolphins, each of which was taught a different artificial language. The dolphin named Phoenix learned a language of machine produced, whistle-like tones that she heard through an underwater speaker. Each tone stood for a different word. Another dolphin, named Ake (short for Akaekamai), learned a language made up of arm gestures given by a trainer standing by the pool. Ake had to raise her head from the water to see the commands.

One of Herman's most important goals was to find out if dolphins could understand syntax. For this reason, he gave the two languages very different structure. In Phoenix's language of whistles, a command was put together this way: direct object [the object Phoenix should do something with] + action + indirect object [where she should take the object]. The word order in Ake's language was indirect object + direct object + action.

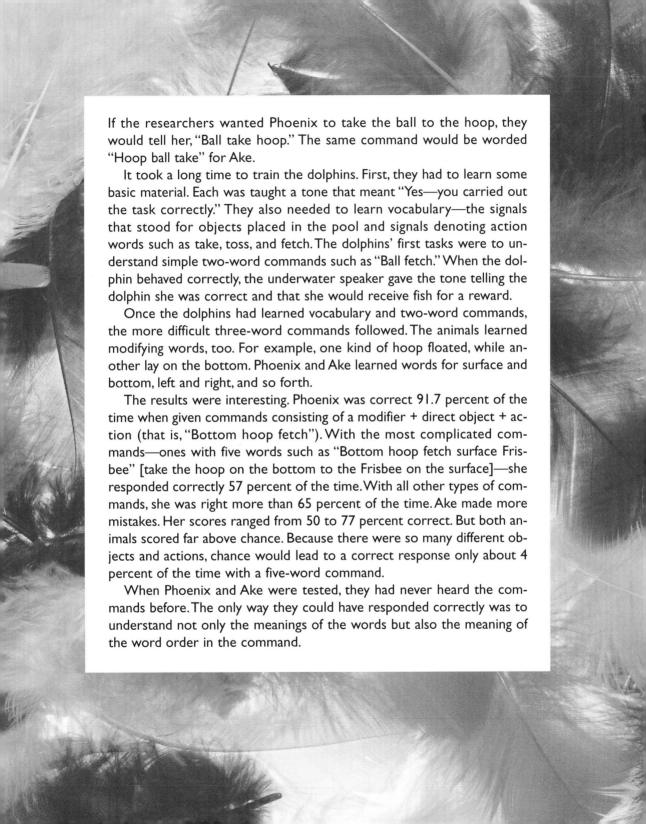

If the researchers wanted Phoenix to take the ball to the hoop, they would tell her, "Ball take hoop." The same command would be worded "Hoop ball take" for Ake.

It took a long time to train the dolphins. First, they had to learn some basic material. Each was taught a tone that meant "Yes—you carried out the task correctly." They also needed to learn vocabulary—the signals that stood for objects placed in the pool and signals denoting action words such as take, toss, and fetch. The dolphins' first tasks were to understand simple two-word commands such as "Ball fetch." When the dolphin behaved correctly, the underwater speaker gave the tone telling the dolphin she was correct and that she would receive fish for a reward.

Once the dolphins had learned vocabulary and two-word commands, the more difficult three-word commands followed. The animals learned modifying words, too. For example, one kind of hoop floated, while another lay on the bottom. Phoenix and Ake learned words for surface and bottom, left and right, and so forth.

The results were interesting. Phoenix was correct 91.7 percent of the time when given commands consisting of a modifier + direct object + action (that is, "Bottom hoop fetch"). With the most complicated commands—ones with five words such as "Bottom hoop fetch surface Frisbee" [take the hoop on the bottom to the Frisbee on the surface]—she responded correctly 57 percent of the time. With all other types of commands, she was right more than 65 percent of the time. Ake made more mistakes. Her scores ranged from 50 to 77 percent correct. But both animals scored far above chance. Because there were so many different objects and actions, chance would lead to a correct response only about 4 percent of the time with a five-word command.

When Phoenix and Ake were tested, they had never heard the commands before. The only way they could have responded correctly was to understand not only the meanings of the words but also the meaning of the word order in the command.

Dolphins, like these at the Shedd Aquarium in Chicago, are easy to train to do spectacular stunts.

they are saying or doing, even though they can respond to unique combinations of symbols appropriately and, in some cases, construct sentences they have never used or heard before. Kanzi is just "going through a bag of tricks in order to get things," according to Dr. Herbert Terrace, one of the sharpest critics of animal language experiments. He claims that "If a child did exactly what the best chimpanzee did, the child would be thought of as disturbed." But then, scientists like Dr. Sue Savage-Rumbaugh have used different methods with their animals than would be used with human children, partly to avoid criticism like that given to the Gardners' work!

Now that we know animals can use what could be called simple language to communicate with us, some linguists have decided to change their definitions. They say that the essence of language is not the ability to recognize words as symbols, to understand them when combined in unique ways, and to create simple sentences. Rather, they say true language is the ability to go beyond simple combinations of symbols like words or markings on computer keys to create ever more complex sentences.

Interacting Intelligently

There is probably no way to avoid the inherent contradiction involved in language work with animals. By definition, language involves the interaction of at least two living things, the one giving the message and the one receiving it and responding. The process of language learning is interactive and therefore cannot ever be investigated purely by the methods of objective science.

When humans communicate, we use more than just words to get the message across. We also use more than what someone says to interpret the message. If someone says "I'm fine" in a sad voice, you know he or she doesn't really feel fine. If you ask a person if he or she remembered to do a chore and the person looks away while answering quickly, "Of course I did," you will be suspicious as to whether the truth is being told.

Scientists have also shown the importance of personal interaction in animal learning. One reason Kanzi, the bonobo, learned so well was that he interacted socially with people as he was learning rather than just using an isolated keyboard. We've seen that a young songbird won't learn the songs of other species from recordings. But if the bird is isolated from its own kind and has a companion from a different species, it may learn to sing the "foreign" song quite well. This direct interaction makes it possible for the young bird to learn a strange song.

Irene Pepperberg has shown a similar situation with parrots. She used three teaching methods—audiotape, videotape, and live human tutors—to try to get two young grey parrots to use

Killer whales, like these being trained at Marine World Africa USA, are intelligent animals that use their own special language for communication.

English language labels for objects. Neither bird learned from either kind of tape, but both did learn from the live tutors. A key element for vocal learning is interaction, the opportunity to communicate back and forth. This should really come as no surprise—after all, communication is the whole point of the vocalizations! Another scientist got similar results using starlings. Only when the birds could interact with human tutors or tutors of another bird species did the starlings learn to make the appropriate sounds.

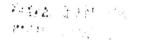

Chapter 6

Talking Parrots

Parrots use vocal communication in a special way that makes them especially prone to learning to "talk." Choosing a mate is serious business, especially if the relationship will be long term, as it is with parrots. Mates need to be counted on to do their part in raising a family. Not just anyone will do. When parrots choose mates, they interact with one another, chattering back and forth and developing their own special "language" that differs from that used by other parrot couples. This intimate chatting is called dueting. By learning and communicating in their own, unique sound combinations, parrot mates recognize one another immediately and solidify their bond.

Just as with humans, parrots may compete with one another for a potential mate, resulting in rivalry. If two males are vying for the favors of one female, each will do his best to attract her attention. She will respond most enthusiastically to the male who impresses her the most.

This capacity to create unique sounds, combined with the desire to please its mate, produces the famous ability of parrots to "talk." For generations, people have been teaching their pet parrots to say things like "Ahoy mate" and "Polly wants a cracker." But usually, the parrots aren't connecting any particular meaning to the sounds they make. Over the years, some people tried without success to find a way of getting parrots to use words as labels for objects and actions. Now and then, an individual parrot showed that it could make the connection between sound and meaning. But attempts to train birds systematically failed.

Teaching Meaning

When Irene began to work with Alex, she devised a method of training that took advantage of the parrot's natural dueting behavior. During the early 1970s, another scientist (Dietmar Todt of Freiburg, Germany) had taken advantage of the natural rivalry in how parrots choose a mate in order to quickly teach parrots to mimic human speech. Two people talked back and forth while the parrot looked on. One person was the parrot's trainer, to whom the bird was already attached. He played the role of the mate. The other person took the role of the parrot rival. The trainer might ask the other person (in German), "What do you say early in the day?" "Good morning," the "rival" might answer. Then the trainer would shower the rival with attention. When the parrot chimed in, mimicking the rival, it got the "mate's" attention instead. Using this method, the scientist could get a parrot to learn its part in a duet in as little as three days. However, the parrots weren't expected to associate meaning with the words and phrases they learned.

Beginning in 1977, Irene began to train Alex using the dueting method. But she modified the procedure in important ways so Alex could develop associations between words and their meanings. Two people interacted to help the parrot learn. But there are key differences between Irene's method and the earlier one. Instead of one person always acting as the trainer, or potential mate, and the other as the trainee, the two people

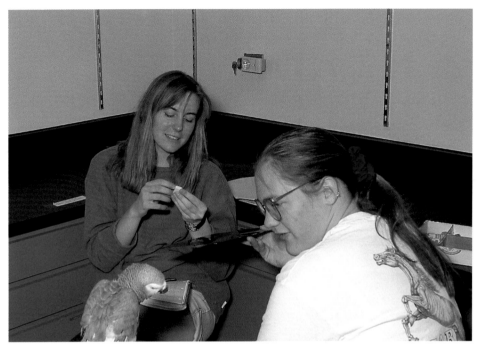

Cyndi Baker and Karter Neal (right) use the model/rival method to teach Alex. Cyndi has given a correct response and is showing great pleasure that Karter has given her the object to play with.

took turns as trainer and trainee so that Alex could see that communication goes both ways. The trainee was acting both as a model for the parrot and as a rival, so the method was called the model/rival approach.

The objects and actions for which words are taught are things of potential interest to a parrot, thus motivating Alex to learn. For example, Alex likes to play with corks, so *cork* was one of his earliest words. Once Alex used a word correctly, he got to play with the object that the word labeled. Not only did this procedure reward Alex, it also provided an opportunity to strengthen the association of the object with the word. If Alex became inattentive or got sloppy, the trainers would threaten to leave. The social interaction itself is a reward for a parrot, and Alex would try to coax a departing trainer into returning by saying things like "Come here" and "Want tickle."

Here's an example of an early training session with Alex. I refers to Irene, B to another trainer, Bruce Rosen, and A to Alex. Bruce and Irene are trying to get Alex to associate the word *pasta* with a piece of macaroni and to pronounce the word well.

I: Bruce, what's this?

B: Pasta (loudly).

I: Good boy! Here you go. (Hands over a piece of pasta.)

A: (Interrupting) Ah-ah.

B: Do you want this, Alex? What is it?

A: Pah-ah.

B: Better. . . .

A: Pah-ah.

B: No. Irene, what's this?

I: Pah-ah.

B: Better!

I: Pas-ta (emphasizing the s and t).

B: That's right, tell me what it is again. (Offers pasta.)

I: Pasta! (Takes pasta.) Pasta! (Alex stretches from his perch on top of the cage and appears to reach for pasta.)

A: Pa!

I: Better—what is it?

A: Pah-ah.

I: Better!

A: Pah-ta.

I: Okay, here's the pasta. Good try.

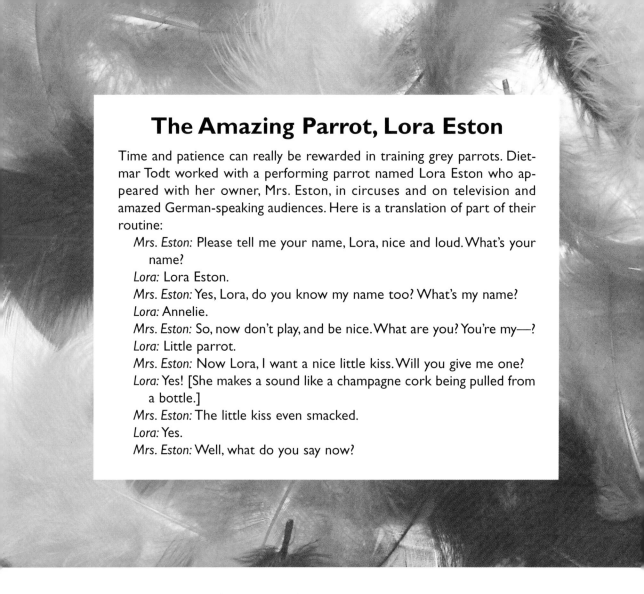

The Amazing Parrot, Lora Eston

Time and patience can really be rewarded in training grey parrots. Dietmar Todt worked with a performing parrot named Lora Eston who appeared with her owner, Mrs. Eston, in circuses and on television and amazed German-speaking audiences. Here is a translation of part of their routine:

Mrs. Eston: Please tell me your name, Lora, nice and loud. What's your name?

Lora: Lora Eston.

Mrs. Eston: Yes, Lora, do you know my name too? What's my name?

Lora: Annelie.

Mrs. Eston: So, now don't play, and be nice. What are you? You're my—?

Lora: Little parrot.

Mrs. Eston: Now Lora, I want a nice little kiss. Will you give me one?

Lora: Yes! [She makes a sound like a champagne cork being pulled from a bottle.]

Mrs. Eston: The little kiss even smacked.

Lora: Yes.

Mrs. Eston: Well, what do you say now?

You can see that this method requires a lot of patience on the part of the trainers. At the beginning, it took hours and hours to get Alex to say just a few words correctly and to associate them with the appropriate objects and actions. His first word was *paper*, and it took two weeks for him to learn the *a-er* sound combination. But once he got the idea, learning new

Lora: That was great!

Mrs. Eston: But Lora, can you whistle too?

Lora: Yes.

Mrs. Eston: Then show us. Please, Lora, whistle.

[Lora then whistles the melody to a familiar German song entitled, "You're cuckoo, kiddo."]

Mrs. Eston: Now that's rude, you're being naughty.

Lora: No.

Mrs. Eston: Yes, you are naughty.

Lora: No!

The routine went on with Lora mimicking the sound of an alarm clock, the deep barking of a big dog, the high-pitched yapping of a small dog, and so forth, concluding with whistling a part in a waltz played by an orchestra, always chiming in at the right time. At the end of the piece, Lora would add an extra note, bringing laughter from the audience.

Lora Eston's training for her long and impressive routine consisted of slowly and patiently building a dueting routine with Mrs. Eston, using the rival method. Even people who raised and trained grey parrots were amazed by the performance.

words came more quickly. By 1988, 11 years after training began, Alex could name 30 objects, 7 colors, and 5 shapes. By the early 1990s, he had added more than 10 more objects to his vocabulary, as well as the names for 5 different kinds of materials and the numbers up to 6.

Chapter 7

Bird Smarts

Language is only one aspect of what we call intelligence. Tool use, a good memory, and the ability to recognize categories of objects are aspects of intelligence that can be scientifically tested more easily than language skills. Some birds have amazing abilities in these areas.

Using Tools

Perhaps the best known tool-using birds are finches living on the Galápagos Islands that use cactus spines or twigs to pry out hidden insects. The finches become experts at their task. The basic behavior appears to be inborn rather than learned, however, because all members of the species perform the behavior without learning it from other finches or figuring it out on their own.

Birds can learn to use tools, too. In laboratory experiments, other kinds of finches have learned, by watching birds in nearby cages, how to use twigs to get at food.

Members of the crow family (ravens, crows, jays, and magpies) are among the most intelligent of birds. These birds can figure out on their own how to use tools. In Texas, a scientist observed green jays pick up small sticks and use them to pry loose bark from trees to reach insects underneath. A northern jay in captivity figured out how to use short sticks to reach otherwise unobtainable food.

These intelligent birds have figured out other ways to solve the problem of getting a meal, too. Magpies often gang up on other animals to steal their food. One magpie will peck at the tail feathers of a young bald eagle that has snagged a fish, for example. When the eagle turns around to get the magpie, the other magpie hops in quickly and steals the fish.

A group of Finnish fishermen learned to their amazement just how good hooded crows can be at obtaining food. The fishermen left baited lines in ice holes. When they returned to see if they had caught any fish, they found instead that crows were at work stealing their fish. The birds were grabbing the lines with their beaks, then backing up to pull the lines out of the water. After pulling the line out a bit, the crow would walk forward, holding the line under its feet as it moved so the line wouldn't slip. At the edge of the ice hole, the bird would grab

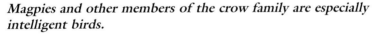

Magpies and other members of the crow family are especially intelligent birds.

the line again in its beak and pull backward again. The crow repeated these actions until the fish was within reach.

Amazing Memory

A particularly intelligent member of the crow family, Clark's nutcracker, combines learning with a fabulous memory in order to survive in the cold, snowy mountains where it lives. If you've ever camped high up in the western mountains, you've probably met this noisy grey bird with black and white markings on its wings. Clark's nutcracker is a fast learner and quickly becomes a campground pest, hanging out in trees overhanging picnic tables and grabbing snacks from human campers, earning its nickname, the camp robber.

But the camp robber has more impressive talents. Summer is short and food is scarce during the long, snowy northern winter. In order to survive, the nutcracker must store its food. In the fall, a nutcracker busies itself collecting pine seeds and storing as many as 33,000 of them in as many as 7,500 small batches in the ground or in tree crevices. The bird has to remember at least a third of these storage sites to last through several months of winter. The task is made more difficult by the snow cover that changes the landscape radically from the way it appeared in the fall.

Scientists Alan Kamil and Russell Balda have studied Clark's nutcracker in the laboratory to test its amazing memory. Even in the unnatural environment of a laboratory, a nutcracker can remember for a month, with 90 percent accuracy, where it stashed nuts on a sand-covered floor. It can do this even when there are no landmarks close to the stashes. In the wild, the birds will move pine cones and pebbles on top of their stashes or hide their food within a few inches of a landmark such as a rock.

The Clark's nutcracker has an amazing memory.

Think about it. Could you remember several thousand locations of hidden items over a period of weeks or months? We humans are always forgetting where we stashed things. Just remembering the next morning where the Easter eggs were hidden is hard for us! We have trouble remembering the simplest things—locker combinations, phone numbers, people's names. But then, our survival doesn't require that we remember so well. Nutcrackers couldn't have survived in their environment generation after generation if they had not developed their remarkable memory.

Recognizing Categories

For a long time, scientists considered the ease with which humans could place things in categories a hallmark of our especially intelligent brains. One beginning textbook for students of mental processes proclaims, "One of the most pervasive aspects of human thought is the tendency to divide the world into categories." Science writer M. Hunt wrote in *Self* magazine, "One of the really astounding things the mind does, apparently effortlessly, is group similar things and make a concept of them.

This is something that, as far as we know, no animal can do." But that was written before scientists like Harvard's R. J. Herrnstein began studying the mental abilities of pigeons.

Pigeons look like quite ordinary birds, and perhaps they are. But since they are easy to tame and raise in captivity, pigeons make very good experimental subjects. Experiments with pigeons have given scientists new respect for the minds of birds. First of all, the memory of pigeons is impressive. Dr. Herrnstein and his associates showed that a laboratory pigeon could learn to recognize 320 randomly chosen photographic slides and can remember 160 slides for two years or more.

If pigeons could remember images so well, perhaps they could also recognize categories, which might enable them to classify the slides mentally and therefore remember them better. Dr. Herrnstein and his colleagues trained pigeons to respond to slides with images that fit into certain categories. For example, birds were shown 40 slides of all sorts of trees—trees with wide leaves and ones with spiky needles, bare winter trees and lush green summer ones. The location and prominence of the trees

Pigeons may be common, ordinary birds, but they are capable of surprising tasks involving categorization and memory.

varied. Sometimes the trees stood out obviously from the background; in other pictures, they were just a part of the background. The slides with trees were mixed randomly with 40 treeless slides chosen to be as much like the others as possible, except for the missing trees.

Each bird had a computer key in front of it while it viewed the slides. If the pigeon pecked at the key when no tree showed in the slide, nothing happened. But if it pecked at the key when a tree slide was shown, it was likely to get a food pellet. By the second session, three of the four birds tested had already figured out that they should peck when the slide showed trees. The fourth bird caught on by the fifth session.

The scientists knew, however, that pigeons have excellent memories. Maybe the birds had just memorized which slides brought food and which didn't. The next experiment ruled out memory. The birds viewed 80 slides of underwater scenes, half with fish and half without. Some slides without fish showed a diver, turtle, or other living thing. The scientists used two groups of pigeons. One got pellets for recognizing fish, just as in the tree experiment. The other group was rewarded for pecking when particular slides appeared. Some of the rewarded slides had fish and some didn't, so those pigeons had to memorize which slides might bring them a pellet. The experiments clearly showed that birds can recognize categories: the pigeons trained to respond to the concept of fish learned twice as fast as the group that had to memorize individual slides.

Japanese scientists confirmed the work of the American scientists in a clever way. They showed pigeons slides of paintings by the artists Claude Monet and Pablo Picasso and rewarded the pigeons for selecting the work of one artist or the other. After about 20 sessions, the birds were pecking correctly around

The pigeon brain may be small, but it is powerful.

90 percent of the time. The birds had developed not only an eye for a Picasso or a Monet, but a concept of the different styles of the two artists. Picasso was a cubist painter, while Monet was an impressionist. When the scientists showed the birds slides from the impressionist Renoir and the cubist Braque, birds trained to peck at Monet pecked at both new Monet paintings and those of Renoir, while the Picasso-trained birds chose Braques as well as new Picassos. The pigeons could recognize elements of the painting styles humans call cubist and impressionist, all with their little "bird brains."

Life in the Wild

Many people are surprised to find that birds such as pigeons can carry out such refined sorting of images into categories. In fact, other experiments with the pigeons showed they could set up a category, such as leaves typical of one kind of tree, with just one image. Imagine a bird living in its natural environment, one that feeds on a variety of foods. If it is to survive, this bird needs to be able to tell the difference between food and not-food. The bird pecks at a particular type of seed and finds it is edible. That image goes into the food category. From then on, when the bird sees a seed that looks like that, it can eat it right away, and it can scan the ground for seeds that look like that. In the same way, if it pecks at something that is not food, items that look like that can be put into the not-food category and ignored from then on. The bird need not waste time pecking over and over again at those items that will not nourish it. It is reasonable to think that birds would also set up other categories, such as shelter and not-shelter, predator and not-predator.

When birds like this red-shafted flicker concentrate on just one kind of food, they are more efficient in their foraging.

Chapter 8

Other Aspects of Intelligence

Some sorts of intelligent mental activity, such as the ability to count or to form concepts and make comparisons, are harder to get at without a way of communicating directly with the experimental subject. That's where Alex and Irene come in. Once Alex learned to associate words with objects and attributes (like colors or the material something is made of), Irene could test for a number of mental abilities.

This dialog Alex and Irene had for a television interview shows how he can use his grasp of words to indicate what sorts of discriminations his brain can make. As she talks, Irene is holding up a green plastic key and a red metal one.

I: Hey, tell me how many.

A: Two.

I: You're right! (She hands him the red key, which he mouths and drops.) Good parrot!

A: Wanna nut.

I: Yes, you can have a nut. (She gives him one.) Now look. (She holds up the keys again.) Tell me what's different.

A: Color.

I: Good parrot, you're right, different color. (She hands him

Karter shows Alex a blue key, and he names it.

the metal key, which he mouths and drops, then the green one, which he drops quickly. She picks them up.)

I: Now look, tell me, what color bigger?

A: Green.

I: Green, good boy, green bigger. Good parrot. Oh, you're a good boy today. Three different questions on the same objects—good parrot!

In this simple exchange, Alex has successfully identified the quantity, two, and has shown he can recognize differences such as color, and comparisons such as the concept of bigger and smaller. Not only that, he has shown that he can understand what kind of question is being asked. When asked a question about quantity, he answers appropriately. He also knows when the question deals with differences and when it involves a comparison.

More about Categories

The experiments with pigeons showed birds can easily recognize categories. But are they just dividing the world into items that are included in a category, such as food, and those that are not in the category, like not-food?

Alex's ability to answer questions with English words allows Irene to find out more about at least one bird's ability to use categories. Alex can recognize different instances within a particular category. For example, he knows there is a category called "color." For Alex, color includes rose (red), green, blue, yellow, grey (grey or black), purple, and orange. He also recognizes the category "shape" that contains two-corner (football shaped), three-corner (triangle), and so forth on up to six-corner. The materials ("matter") he is familiar with are cork, wood, hide (rawhide), rock (things made of Play-Doh), paper, chalk, and wool (pompon or piece of felt).

Alex recognizes that the same object can belong to different categories such as color and shape. Alex is very good at this task. When asked to categorize an object by color or shape, he can do so with 85.5 percent accuracy.

Getting Complicated

Alex has also mastered the more complicated task of recognizing which object fits into two different categories at the same time. For example, instead of being asked a question such as,

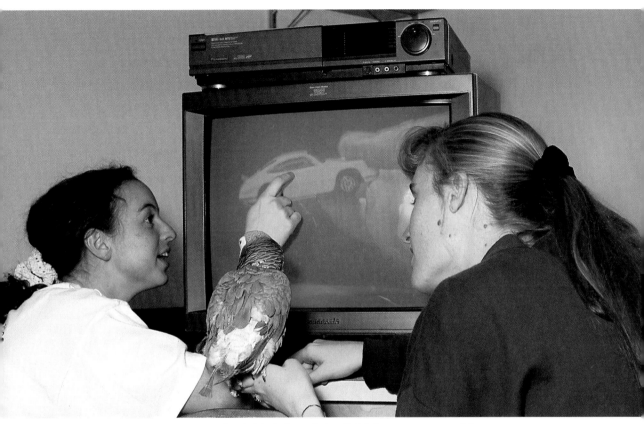

Students Kris Stanford (right) and April Mahay try to get Alex to recognize a toy car ("truck" to Alex) on a TV monitor.

"What matter is (the object that is) green?" Alex is asked something like, "What matter is (the object that is) green and four-cornered?" This question asks that he not only be able to recognize the object that fits into a color and shape category, but also that he identify its place in yet a third category, "matter."

In this set of experiments, Irene chooses seven objects from among one hundred objects made up of various combinations

Karter shows Alex three objects that share two categories (shape and material) but differ in a third (color).

of materials, colors, and shapes. When she decides which objects to display on the tray, Irene has to think carefully about what she is including. For example, the tray might contain the following objects: circular orange wood, two-corner yellow wood, three-corner green wood, five-corner grey wool, five-corner rose hide, five-corner blue paper, five-corner purple wood. Then Alex is asked, "What color is the five-corner wood?" After some thought, he gives the correct response—"Purple."

In the collection of objects were four different wooden objects and four different five-cornered ones. Alex could not get the correct response easily by just guessing, as there were eight choices that fit one or the other of the criteria, five-cornered and wood. But only one object, the purple one, was *both* five-cornered *and* wood. For every question, Irene must be careful to select an assortment of items that allow for one unique answer. If she had included another purple item on the tray, she wouldn't know if Alex had picked the correct item or not when he answered, "Purple."

In this task, Alex is sometimes asked the color of the item, other times the shape, and at still other times the material. So

When Irene showed Alex this assortment of objects and asked, "What material green, Alex?" he answered correctly, "Wood." Then she asked, "How many yellow?" After thinking for a moment, he answered, "Three."

he is quizzed on his ability to combine the categories in all possible ways to figure out an answer. Alex's success is impressive—he has answered this difficult kind of question correctly 76.5 percent of the time.

Comparisons

Scientists tried a number of times to investigate whether birds could understand the concept of "same" and "different." They had little success until Alex came along. Again, his ability to answer in words made the work much easier. Just as he can recognize when items fit into particular categories, such as green in color, so he knows when two objects are different, like when he was asked in the above dialog what was different about the two keys. He can recognize sameness and difference in color, shape, and material of items. And he can do it even with items that are unfamiliar to him. If he is asked, "What's same?" and the items do not share a trait, Alex will answer, "None."

As he demonstrated in the dialog above, Alex can also make other comparisons, such as bigger versus smaller.

Knowing Numbers

Over many experimental sessions, Alex has shown he can identify quantities of items shown to him on the tray. For example, as part of one session, Irene placed seven objects on a tray. She asked a number of different questions, each requiring a different sort of mental ability. One question was, "How many yellow?" Alex took his time looking over the colorful display of objects, then answered, "Three." He was right. He was able to pick out and recognize the number of yellow objects, even though they were different in size, shape, and material. In experiments like this, Alex has been able to identify quantities up

Irene and Alex work on a task involving numbers.

to six, even on a tray cluttered with many objects of different shapes, colors, and materials.

When Irene focused on Alex's ability to enumerate objects, he performed as well as adult human subjects in a similar study. In these experiments, Alex was shown a collection of items that varied in two object categories and two color categories, such as red and blue cars and keys. Irene would then ask a question such as, "How many red car?" Alex was correct 83.3 percent of the time. Before Alex, scientists had no idea that a bird could perform such a complex task so successfully.

Fighting Boredom

Just like a person, Alex has a job. And sometimes he doesn't feel like working. Answering the same kinds of questions over and over again can be very boring for an intelligent animal like Alex, and he's been doing this for years. Boredom is a hazard with any intelligent animal. While science requires repetition and consistency in results to consider something proven, intelligent animals balk at boring repetition. Sometimes, they show their boredom through their behavior. One chimp who used ASL responded to a particularly boring session by making signs in his ear rather than in front of his body as if to say, "This is really boring." When Alex, who has already shown he can recognize quantities, decides in one session to answer "Four" to every number question *except* those for which "four" is the correct answer, he is probably communicating his boredom with the task.

Alex may be an adult parrot, but in some ways he is very much like a human child. Not only is his mental ability at a child's level, his emotional maturity is similar to that of a very young child. This helps in training, for Alex easily becomes jealous, and he wants plenty of attention from Irene and her students. But it can also result in problems, for Alex can be stubborn, pecking at the tray used to display items, demanding tidbits when he's supposed to be working, or apparently giving wrong answers on purpose when he doesn't want to work.

Irene and Alex look over the huge collection of objects and toys she uses to try to keep him interested in his work.

Alex likes to play with new objects, like this film container.

Irene does what she can to help keep Alex from getting so bored that he won't work. He is especially bored when asked to work with objects that he is completely familiar with. He lets Irene know by naming favorite objects on the tray and grabbing them before he's even asked a question or biting at the tray. So, when possible, Irene uses objects Alex hasn't seen before which might pique his curiosity. He pays more attention then and performs better on the tasks.

Another way to keep his interest is to mix up the different tasks during a session. Alex can also get other rewards besides just playing with the object. If he asks for a nut or a cork, a favorite toy, after a correct response, he is likely to get one. Alex has also learned to say, "Wanna go tree," and "Go see tree." That means he wants to go upstairs to a window where he can look outside and see the trees.

Alex has also had vacations lasting from a few days to months when he hasn't been tested. Then, when work resumes, he is likely to be more interested.

Alex Goes to the Hospital

Alex can even use his knowledge of word meanings to communicate spontaneously. In September of 1990, Irene almost lost Alex to a serious lung infection. It was a scary time. They tried to treat him at home in the laboratory, but it just didn't work. Alex refused to take his medicine, and one important treatment involved a procedure that just couldn't be carried out in the lab. So, reluctantly, Irene took Alex to the veterinary hospital. He had never spent a night in a strange place.

Before she left him that afternoon, Irene tried to reassure the frightened parrot. But as she headed for the door, Alex called out, "Come here. I love you. I'm sorry. Wanna go back." Alex was doing his best to make Irene stay with him. Irene felt bad, but she had no choice but to leave Alex at the hospital.

While Alex was in the hospital, Irene had to visit every day; otherwise, Alex wouldn't eat. After the infection was cured, Alex had to be flown to Florida for surgery to remove an air sac damaged by the infection. (Birds have extensions of the lungs, called air sacs, that branch into other parts of the body.) Only two veterinarians in the country were qualified at that time to perform this delicate operation. Fortunately, Alex came through just fine.

Alex got the lung infection from contaminated bedding that had seemed harmless. Since Alex's illness, Irene is especially careful about what is brought into the lab that might carry a disease.

Chapter 9

A Day in Irene's Life

Irene and Alex both live busy lives, but Irene's is much more complicated. In addition to working with Alex, she is responsible for teaching university students, writing scientific papers, running her laboratory, helping graduate students with their experiments, and taking care of Kyo and Grif, the two young African greys who are beginning to learn how to "talk."

Irene's day begins at 6:30, when she gets up and prepares to go to work. While she runs errands for Alex, such as shopping for treats, students arrive at the lab at 8:00 to feed the birds and clean the cages. Work sessions begin at 9:00. Each session is a half hour long, and half-hour breaks are alternated with work sessions. Alex and the other parrots work with a number of different students as well as with Irene. Anyone who is involved with the parrots must be patient, have a good sense of humor, and not mind feeling a bit ridiculous at times.

Parrots may be able to learn to speak, understand, and use words in much the same way human children do, but teaching them takes long hours and a great deal of patience on the part of the trainers. What comes naturally to humans may be difficult for parrots because of the way they interact with their world. Connecting the sounds they make with very specific objects and actions in their environment, other than their fellow

Irene's three subjects—Kyo (left), Alex (on her hand), and Grif (on her shoulder)—keep Irene very busy.

African greys, may not be something they normally do in the wild. Scientists believe African greys, like vervet monkeys, have predator alarm calls that may each refer to a particular type of predator. And there is evidence they have a general "good food" call they use when they find an abundant food source. But they probably don't have calls that indicate specific foods such as palm nuts or maize. If their natural calls do not indicate such details, making the connection between the vocalizations they are taught in the laboratory and specific objects and actions could be especially difficult, even though it is based on talents they already possess.

Irene gets to the lab around 9:30 and checks to make sure everything is running smoothly. Sometime during the morning she spends time with each of the birds, tickling them, letting them perch on her shoulder, and giving them treats.

Time to Work

For each of Alex's work sessions, a list of tasks is made out ahead of time. Each session consists of a mixture of different tasks—comparisons, numerical problems, and so forth. Each session, then, tests a variety of mental abilities. Each day, Irene conducts one session each with Alex and Grif. The other sessions are handled by students.

Here's part of a session with students Karter and Cyndi. At first, Alex is being stubborn, saying "truck" for a blue plastic key. When he's given a blue metal key, he answers "key" right away. Part of this session is teaching Alex to recognize the shapes of plastic numbers. Karter shows Alex a number one. He

Karter has to be patient while she teaches Alex to recognize the numeral '5.'

says, "Four." Cyndi then gives the right answer, and Karter enthusiastically tells her, "Good parrot," as she strokes the plastic number one happily. When Alex gets the wrong answer again, the students act very disappointed in him.

Next, they show him a plastic number five, and Alex says "Four." Cyndi gets all excited about saying "Five," and Karter rewards her with a nut, which she eats happily. Then they ask Alex a trick question. They show him two identical yellow keys and ask, "What's different?" For a while, Alex doesn't answer but finally responds, "None." He wants a nut, but they don't give it yet. When he answers the next question correctly right off the bat and then says "Wanna nut," they reward him with the nut.

Karter uses Alex as a model for Grif, helping him learn "paper."

Alex does a session each day as a model for Grif and another as a model for Kyo. Grif and Kyo's other sessions involve learning new words, working with video experiments, and learning numbers.

Hanging Out

Between sessions, Alex and the other birds get to hang out in the main laboratory room with the students. All day long, people come and go from the laboratory area. In front of the main door is a pan of antiseptic solution. Everyone must dip the bottoms of their shoes in the solution before entering the lab. The air is also specially treated to keep germs to a minimum. Alex and the other birds must be protected from getting sick.

The atmosphere in the main room is quite social, which the parrots enjoy. After all, in the wild they belong to big, noisy flocks. Alex perches on the back of a chair most of the time, watching what's going on, and occasionally announcing, "Wanna nut," or "Wanna go shoulder." Irene and the students talk to Alex and stroke him, especially when he says, "Want tickle."

A favorite activity for Alex is getting a shower. One of the students takes a spray bottle and squirts him with water. Alex runs up to the bottle, runs away, then hops back again and pecks at it. He fluffs his feathers, shakes like a wet dog, and spreads his wings and flaps them. Then he runs toward the bottle again and chirps. Even though he can talk in human language, Alex can still sound like a bird.

The Day Goes On

Irene teaches a class from 11:00 to 12:00. During the noon lunch break, students eat their lunches in the lab while Irene answers mail and returns phone calls. From 1:00 to 3:00, she has her sessions with Alex and with Grif, playing with the birds between sessions. Irene's work with Alex involves whatever he's learning that is new. When Irene works with Grif, she tests him to see what he has learned and how well he understands it.

During the late afternoon, Irene confers with students while

Kris Glaspey gives Alex a shower.

other students finish up any remaining sessions with the parrots. An important part of Irene's job is helping the graduate students with their research and advising them on how best to carry out their experiments. After that, while Irene finishes her desk work, the students clean up the lab and give the parrots fresh food and water. Then the students leave, but not Irene. She stays in the lab and keeps the birds company while she eats her dinner, then works writing scientific papers while Alex and Grif keep her company. At 7:30, Irene puts Alex to bed, while Grif stays up until 8:30. After the birds are in their cages for the night, Irene continues her desk work until she leaves at around 11:00. Then the next morning, it's up again at 6:30 to start a new day.

Chapter 10

Into the Future

Irene is determined to find out just how much a parrot is able to learn. Her latest work with Alex is teaching him the shapes of numbers and the sounds of letters. When he's shown an S, he knows to say "SSSSS." Add an H and he responds, "SHH." Alex has shown that he understands comparisons like bigger and smaller. He's learning the concepts of big, middle, and little, when given objects of different sizes. Even though Alex is about 20 years old, he could still have many more years of learning and showing how intelligent and complex the brain of a parrot is.

The Next Generation

Irene, Alex, and the students work on training Kyo and Grif, using the same methods that worked with Alex. Irene is hoping that using Alex as a model/rival may help the young birds learn faster. Grif learned *wood* in sessions where Alex was the model, and he learned it faster than he learned *nail* from two humans. Irene is using Alex to teach Grif and Kyo more words. In time, Irene will know if the young birds learn better from Alex or from people.

In general, work with Kyo goes slowly. Irene got Kyo when he was over three months old. She thinks he may have a

Irene and Alex help Grif learn "wood."

problem akin to an attention disorder in a human. He is skittish about being handled and has a hard time concentrating during his work sessions. But Irene got Grif when he was only a few weeks old and started working with him almost immediately. Whenever Irene and her students hand an item to Grif, they say its name. In this way, Grif learned right from the start that objects have names. He's also heard the scientists training Alex. At 17 months of age, Grif knows how to say *paper, nail,* and *wood*. He learned to say *wood* just by listening to Alex. Like human babies, young parrots babble, using sounds they've heard during the day. If you listen to a human baby's babbling, you can often hear what sound like words mixed in with the baby sounds. When Grif babbles, he intersperses the words *three* and *four* with his bird calls, and sometimes says *key*.

Grif's Accomplishments

Even though Grif is less than two years old, he has already been the subject of an interesting study. Psychologists and other scientists who study animal behavior are interested in how aspects of behavior that involve thought develop as an animal grows up. They also compare the development of behavior in different species. That's not an easy task—how do you compare such different creatures as a parrot, a dog, and a chimpanzee?

One mental task that can be compared relatively easily across species is called object permanence. The Swiss psychologist Piaget studied the ages and stages of intellectual development in children and established tests to show when certain ways of thinking kick in. A young baby reacts to what it sees. If an object that it can see is hidden, the baby doesn't realize the object still exists out of its sight. As the baby gets older, it reaches a stage when it realizes that an object pulled down behind a screen is still there, out of sight. By the time a child is two years old, it can even understand where to look when an object has been moved twice in the following way: The object is put into a container so it can't be seen. Then the container is hidden behind, say, a screen, and the object is removed from the container and placed behind the screen. When the child is shown that the container is empty, it knows to look for the object behind the screen. Piaget called this the earliest part of the final stage, or Stage 6, of object permanence.

Scientists like to use tests of object permanence because it tells something about how sophisticated an animal's brain is and because testing it is straightforward. Chimpanzees, at least some parrots, and possibly dogs can reach Stage 6, but cats, monkeys, ring doves, hamsters, and chickens apparently can't.

Irene had tested Alex's abilities at object permanence, and he had shown he had reached Stage 6 understanding, but he was already an adult bird. Grif gave the scientists an opportunity to test how object permanence develops in at least one young parrot. When Irene got Grif, he was only eight weeks old. He had only a few downy feathers, and he needed to be fed twice a day. Each day as Grif grew up, Irene and her students spent time just playing with him, presenting him with small toys he could chew, throw, or chase, such as wooden spools, beads, plastic animals, cups, pen caps, and so forth.

Sean holds up a nail, as Grif is learning "nail."

To test Grif's understanding of object permanence, the scientists would hide the toys or bits of food and see if Grif could figure out what happened to them. Like Alex, Grif liked so much to play with toys that just getting them was an adequate reward. The experiments on object permanence were carefully conducted over the first year of Grif's life. Irene and her students tracked the ages at which he reached each stage along the way. He reached the earliest part of Stage 6 when he was only a few months old. Although the information from just one individual can't be generalized to the whole species, it is still valuable for comparison with other species and indicates something about the abilities of the animal's brain.

What's Most Important

When I asked Irene what she felt was most important about her work, she stressed three things. First of all, she and Alex have helped show that a bird's brain, which is organized very differently from a human brain, can still perform many of the same mental tasks as a human brain. Work with dolphins, whose brains are put together in still a different way, shows that they can accomplish many of the same tasks as humans and parrots. Getting at how brains actually process information is not easy, but we can hope that future studies will help unravel how these different kinds of brains end up able to think similarly.

Secondly, Irene hopes that when people appreciate just how intelligent birds like parrots are, they will want to protect them and their homes in the wild. Because they are time-consuming to breed in captivity and are very popular as pets, grey parrots are at risk for being removed from the wild. Anyone buying a grey parrot should make sure it is captive bred. He or she must also be ready to make a lifelong commitment of time and love.

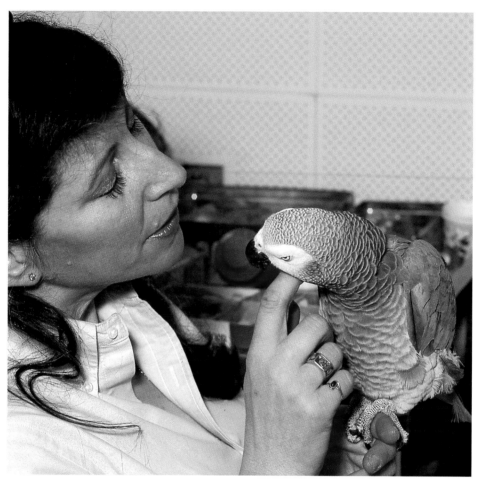

Alex gets a tickle from Irene.

If the habitats where parrots live are saved, many other species that share those habitats will be rescued along with them. The same goes for dolphins—can we ignore the plight of intelligent creatures like parrots and dolphins and just sit by while their habitats are destroyed and the animals disappear?

Helping Children

Irene's third hope is that her work will be useful for people. Her methods for teaching parrots can also be used to help handicapped children learn how to use language. Diane Sherman is an occupational therapist in Monterey, California. She sometimes works with severely handicapped children with the disease cerebral palsy. They cannot control many of their body movements, and they communicate very little with other people. They don't know how to make their needs known and may scream to get attention.

Sherman has used a two-person modeling team in a way similar to what Irene does with parrots to show these children how sounds and hand signals can tell another person what you want. The children enjoy music and rhythm, so Sherman often uses the song "The Itsy Bitsy Spider" as a starting point in therapy. She sings the song, using the hand movements that go along with it, and another person tells her when she's finished, "More!" Then Sherman repeats the song. After only a few examples of the model getting what she wants by saying "More," the child gets the idea and tries to mouth the word, coming out with a sound like "Muh." That's good enough for starters, and Sherman will reward the child by repeating the song. As the work progresses, the model will also make incorrect responses that don't lead to getting to hear the song.

Another favorite song is "Wheels on the Bus." Sherman will sing that song, and the model will ask for more. Then Sherman will ask, "Which one do you want?" By this time, there will be a sound and/or a hand signal that indicates each of the two songs. When the model uses the signal for "The Itsy Bitsy Spider," she gets that song. When she uses the one for "Wheels on the Bus," she gets that one. The child catches on very quickly

Children are naturally attracted to animals. That's one reason animals are used to assist with therapy.

and soon is asking for the favorite song, whichever it is.

Once the child understands that sounds and signals can get him or her a desired activity or object, the screaming often stops and the learning begins. By using a modeling system, Sherman and her helpers show the child how specific signals can get specific results. Screaming is no longer necessary.

Sherman owns a grey parrot, Macumi, who often comes to work with her. Macumi knows some words and phrases such as "Hi," "How you doing?" and "What's you doing?" Sherman was having particular trouble getting one boy to talk. No matter how hard she and others tried, he just didn't get the idea of using words to communicate. But he was fascinated by Macumi, who always greeted him with a cheerful "Hi!" One day the boy turned to the parrot and said in a clear voice, "Hi!" Then he began saying "Hi" to everyone he saw—he'd discovered the power of words. From then on, he continued to learn other words. He became a real chatterbox, thanks to Macumi.

The Future for Grey Parrots

The grey parrot is not currently considered an endangered species. In Ghana, for example, there are still thousands of grey parrots. But years ago there were many more, indicating that more are taken from the wild than can be replaced through breeding. Without some control of trade, the grey parrot could join so many other species on the endangered list.

The illegal trade in wild birds in general is a serious conservation problem. Birds are trapped in large numbers and sent to countries like the United States, where they are sold as pets. International rules about how many birds can be caught in a single country are easy to get around because most countries don't have the money to police the wild bird trade. For example, thousands of grey parrots are trapped illegally in Ghana and the Ivory Coast every year. They are smuggled into nearby countries such as Togo, Mali, and Senegal that have few if any grey parrots of their own, then shipped from there to the United States.

So little is known about the ecology and breeding of wild grey parrots that it is difficult to know how many can be captured without affecting the wild population. Studies of these birds in the wild are therefore very important.

The hyacinth macaw, largest parrot of all, is highly endangered.

Kyo has beautiful bright red tail feathers.

Fortunately, one of Irene's students, Diana May, is hoping to continue her study of wild grey parrot behavior. Diana wants to find out how this bird's remarkable intelligence and ability to mimic and communicate help it in its natural environment. She also wants to find ways to encourage ecotourism, bringing people into the wild to observe nature. When ecotourism succeeds, it provides jobs for local people, making it easier for wild environments to be preserved. If cutting down trees or illegally capturing wild birds is the only way people can make money to support their families, they will have to do those things. But if they can guide groups of tourists through green forests of tall trees filled with beautiful birds and other animals and make money doing it, then they will have a more rewarding job and help preserve the natural world at the same time.

Alex and Irene

Wherever her research leads her, Irene will always have a special place in her heart for Alex. Not only did he help her learn so much about how the brain of at least one bird works, he has been her friend and companion for almost 20 years.

At the end of the day, Irene puts Alex into his cage and tells him she is leaving.

"I'm going now," she says. "You be good."

"You be good," Alex answers.

"See you tomorrow," says Irene.

"Bye," says Alex.

"Bye," she responds.

"I love you," croaks Alex.

Irene's last words as she goes out the door are, "I love you, too."

Glossary

alarm calls—calls animals such as vervet monkeys use to warn others of the approach of a predator

American Sign Language (ASL)—a sign language for the deaf in which hand gestures, in combination with facial expressions and larger body movements, are used instead of speech

bonobo—a species of chimpanzee *(Pan paniscus)* native to Zaire that has a lighter build than the common chimpanzee. The bonobo is also called the pygmy chimpanzee.

cubism—a style of art, begun in 1907, in which the subject is broken apart and reassembled in an abstract form, usually with geometric shapes

dueting—the interactive process by which pairs of parrots create their own, unique sound combinations for communication

endangered species—a species threatened with extinction

grammar—the rules of speaking or writing a language

habitat—the place or environment where a plant or animal naturally or normally lives and grows

impressionism—an art style, begun in France about 1875, depicting the natural appearances of objects by means of dabs or strokes of primary unmixed colors in order to simulate actual reflected light

inborn—present from birth

lexigram—a geometric symbol that stands for an object or action. Some chimpanzees have been taught to use lexigrams on a keyboard to communicate with scientists.

linguist—a scientist who studies languages

linguistics—the study of human speech

model-rival method—a method of training parrots in which two people interact to help the parrot learn

object permanence—the understanding that an object still exists when it is out of sight. Tests of object permanence can show how sophisticated an animal's brain is.

plumage—the feathers of a bird

syntax—the rules that govern the way words are put together to make phrases and sentences

Index

African grey parrot, 25–28; lifespan, 27; mimicking human speech, 25–26; in nature, 26–28, 89–91; physical description, 26–27; predator alarm calls, 76; range, 26; social interaction and learning, 48–49; trade in, 25, 26, 89–91. *See also* Alex; birds

alarm calls, specific. *See* warning calls, specific

Alex: boredom during training, 71–73; category recognition, 66–70; comparison of objects, 65–66, 70, 81; differences, recognition of, 64–66; emotional maturity, 72; leisure activities, 79; as model for other parrots, 78, 81; numbers and letters, recognition of, 81; quantities, identification of, 70–71; spontaneous communication, 74; training sessions, 51–55, 77–78. *See also* African grey parrot; birds; parrots

American Sign Language (ASL), 34; interpretation of, 37; structure of, 40. *See also* chimpanzee: American Sign Language

Arnie. *See* starlings

ASL. *See* American Sign Language

Bates, Elizabeth, 32–33

birds: category recognition, 60–63; memory, 58–59, 60; mimicking human speech, 12–13, 15, 22, 50–51; social interaction and learning, 12, 47–49; songs, 10–12; territories, 11; tools, use of, 56–58; warning calls for specific predators, 10, 76. *See also* African grey parrot; Alex; parrots; pigeons; starlings

bonobo, 39–41; lexigram keyboard, 39–40; understanding structure of language, 40–41. *See also* chimpanzee

Cheney, Dorothy, 9–10

chimpanzee, 32–38; American Sign Language, 32–35; categorizing objects, 38; lexigram keyboard, 38. *See also* bonobo

Chomsky, Noam, 30–32, 42

Clark's nutcracker. *See* birds: memory

Coon, Adell and Don, 22–24

dolphins, 42, 44–45

dueting. *See* parrots: communication between mates, rival method of training

dueting method. *See* parrots: rival method of training

Eston, Lora and Mrs., 54–55

Gardner, Beatrix and R. Allen, 33–37

Haegeman, Liliane, 31

Herman, Louis, 44–45

Herrnstein, R. J., 60–61

Hoy, Judy, 13–15

intelligence: boredom associated with, 71–72; category recognition, 59–63; factors linked to, 20–21; lifespan and, 21; memory and, 58–59, 60; social behavior and, 21; tools, use of, 56–58. *See also* learning

language: definition of, 29–33, 41–43, 47; "language organ," 30, 31–32, 42–43; messages, interpretation of, 21; processing of, in human brain, 32–33; structure of, 40–41, 44–45; study of, 30–31; teaching to handicapped children, 87, 89; words, recognizing as symbols, 42

learning: generalizing knowledge, 35; social interaction and, 12, 47–49. *See also* intelligence

lexigrams. *See* bonobo, chimpanzee

Marler, Peter, 12
model method in teaching handicapped children, 87, 89
model/rival method. *See* parrots: model/rival method of training

Neville, Helen, 32
Nicki. *See* parrots: appropriate use of words

object permanence: in humans, 83; in parrots, 83–85
objectivity, in scientific experimentation, 35–36, 47

parrots, 16–28; appropriate use of words, 22–24, 74; babbling, 82; and children, 87–89; communication between mates, 50, 51; connecting sounds with meanings, 48–49, 51–52, 75–76; emotional needs, 24; habitats of, 26, 85–86; intelligence, 20–21; lifespan, 20, 21, 27; mimicking human speech, 12–13, 15, 22, 50–51; model/rival method of training, 51–55, 81; object permanence, 83–85; as pets, 15, 21–24; range, 16, 18–19, 26; rival method of training, 51, 54–55; rivalry among, 50; scientific classification, 18–19; social behavior, 20, 21, 53, 79; species of, 16, 18–19. *See also* African grey parrot; Alex; birds
Pepperberg, Irene, 6–8, 85–87; and Alex, 51–55, 64–73, 74, 77, 79, 81; daily routine, 75–77, 79–80; development of model/rival method, 51–52; importance of interaction in teaching parrots, 48–49; work with Grif, 78, 79, 81–85; work with Kyo, 78, 81–82. *See also* Alex
Peters, S., 12

pigeons, 60–63. *See also* birds

rival method. *See* parrots, rival method of training

Savage-Rumbaugh, Duane, 38–41
Savage-Rumbaugh, Sue, 38–41, 43, 46–47
scientific experimentation, 35–36; criticism as part of, 37
sea lions, 42, 43
Seyfarth, Robert, 9–10
Shanker, Stuart, 31
Sherman, Diane, 87, 89
social interaction, role in learning, 12, 47–49
starlings, 12–15; social interaction and learning, 48–49; words, combining into sentences, 13, 15. *See also* birds
syntax. *See* language: structure of

Terrace, Herbert, 46–47
Todt, Dietmar, 51, 54

vervet monkeys. *See* warning calls, specific

warning calls, specific, 9–10; African grey parrot's use of, 76
Washoe, 32–35. *See also* chimpanzee
word order. *See* language: structure of
words. *See* language

*Alex and the author
get acquainted.*

About the Author

Dorothy Hinshaw Patent was born in Minnesota and spent most of her growing-up years in Marin County, California. She has a Ph.D. in zoology from the University of California. Dr. Patent is the author of over 90 nonfiction books for children including *Baby Horses, Dogs: The Wolf Within, Horses,* and *Cattle* from Carolrhoda Books and *Apple Trees* from Lerner Publications. Her books have received a number of awards, including the Golden Kite from the Society of Children's Book Writers and Illustrators and the Children's Choice Award from the International Reading Association. She has two grown sons and lives in Missoula, Montana, with her husband, Greg.

About the Photographer

William Muñoz lives with his wife and son in western Montana. He has been photographing nature for over 20 years. Mr. Muñoz exhibits his photographs at art fairs throughout the USA and has collaborated with Dorothy Patent on numerous critically acclaimed books for children.